OLD GUY, PART ONE

GETTING USED TO OLD AGE AND RETIREMENT

Poems

by

Tom Carnicelli

Old Guy, Part One: Getting Used to Old Age and Retirement
Copyright © 2015 by Tom Carnicelli

This is a work of fiction.

Published by Piscataqua Press
An imprint of RiverRun Bookstore, Inc.
142 Fleet Street | Portsmouth, NH | 03801
www.riverrunbookstore.com
www.piscataquapress.com

Printed in the United States of America

ISBN: 978-1-939739-89-6

TABLE OF CONTENTS

A NOTE TO THE READER

A NOTE TO THE READER.

I've put "Part One" in my title because these poems express my thoughts and feelings during the first year and a half of my being retired. At this stage, a retired old guy is trying to figure out how to make good use of all this extra time he's acquired. He wants to have a good time, but he also wants to accomplish something. Finding that something isn't so easy. I've lost some close relatives and some good friends during this past year and a half, but I've decided not to include poems about death and dying. I want to focus my attention on daily living.

I've grouped these poems in sections. The first three groups provide some sense of chronology, but not, I hope, a sense of resolution. I don't want to suggest that I've become fully comfortable with old age or retirement. I haven't, and perhaps I never will. In the other sections, I look at things I see and do in terms of my new situation. I find that, when you're old and retired, you pay more attention to other old people and, at least in my case, to children, who are also outside the working world.

One favor I would ask is that you don't condemn me for any outrageous attitudes expressed in some of these poems. Please look at these poems as records of various moods, not as my considered opinions now. I'm well aware that some of the comments by my speakers are laughable; please feel free to laugh at them.

T.C

DENIALS

REAL ADULTS

Now that all the real adults
Are in Assisted Living,
People are looking to us.

Sit up straight.
Look like you know
What you're doing.

God, if they only knew.

OLD GUYS

I'm not one of them.

I never wear a baseball cap
Or a team T-shirt or sweatshirt.

I have a full head of hair. I don't
Need to comb it from back to front.

I don't talk about my past exploits.
I try not to talk about the past at all.

You might think I'm old when you see
My white head, but you'd be wrong.

An old man walks slowly, legs apart,
As if he has a big load in his pants.

That's not the way I walk. There's
No load in my pants. No, sir-ree.

A BUNCH OF OLD CROCKS

I

The white heads are flocking to the theater
For the Saturday matinee. They're going to see
The opera, broadcast live from the Met.
I hate being in crowds of old people.
I walk among them reluctantly, wishing
I were invisible, moaning to myself:
"I'm not like these old crocks.
I might look like them,
But inside I'm different."

I'm not much different, I know,
Though my stubborn vanity keeps trying
To make me think so. I'm sure I'm like
These others, both outside and in.
We all find our aging forms misleading;
We all know that what we look like
Can't come near to what we are.
We know that, to the world at large,
All of us are a bunch of old crocks.
And that makes me one, too.

III

And yet, who but a bunch
Of old crocks would go the opera
On a sunny Saturday afternoon?
Who else would go the opera
Any time at all?

FEDORA MAN

With his white hair
And his serious demeanor,
An old guy can look
Distinguished.

Who's to know
That, under that grave exterior,
Is a kid who liked to blow farts
In the bathtub?

An old guy
Must keep up appearances,
Dress in a manner appropriate
To his body's age.

No baseball caps,
No t-shirts with slogans or logos,
Nothing only the young can wear
Without absurdity.

Only a fedora
Suits an old man; only an old man
Can wear one and not be a youngster
Dressed like an adult.

Our fathers wore
Fedoras, and their fathers before them.
An old guy wearing a fedora today is a man
Among men,

Not the kid
He feels like inside, who has made
Scant progress on wisdom's road, but who knows
What a grown-up looks like.

BEING OLD

NAMES

The marketers don't know what to call us.
"Old" is out – much too blunt, apparently.
Nobody would buy an Oldsmobile today,
(Not even your father), and AARP will not
Be changed to AROP any time soon.
"Elderly" is a softer word, but we all know
It's just a way to soften the blow,
Just as we know that "elder statesmen"
Are politicians who have lost power.
"Senior citizen" seems to have had its day,
Though "senior" lives on in discounts.
"Oldster" insults us, making youngsters
The norm and us the imitation.

Let's just stick with "old." I can live
With it well enough. But I'd much rather
Be called an "old guy" than an "old man."
If you're an old man, you're old and frail.
If you're an old guy, you're still a little frisky.

BAD DAY

Today was a bad day.
My feet hurt, and I dragged myself
Around the city at half-speed.
I couldn't seem to read the map -
I kept making wrong turns,
Getting us farther away
From what we'd planned to see.
When we'd get to a famous place,
I couldn't seem to see why
It was special and important.
I didn't particularly enjoy lunch
At a really very nice café,
And I know I was lousy company
The whole long day.

Old age is great when you don't feel old.
Today, I did.

LOOKING OLD

We both noticed it, right away:
"Harry's looking old, isn't he?"
Harry is well into his eighties,
But, two weeks ago, he looked
Just fine. What did we see today?
What is it that makes a person
Suddenly look old?

Perhaps it was his dress.
The black suit was shiny
At the knees and pockets.
There were spots and fuzzies
On the back of his pantlegs,
Where he couldn't see them.
His tie-knot was askew.

Still, it was more than dress.
"He's acting old," we said.
We noticed how it took him
Forever to hang up his coat,
How his speech was bland and tame –
No questionable jokes, no jabs
At the usual foes.

We all have bad days.
Maybe the old Harry will come
Roaring back, exposing this new one
As an imposter. Or maybe not.
Maybe there comes a point
When looking, acting, and being old
Become the same.

13

AUNT HELEN

Denials are futile, as I learned from
A birthday card with a stern Margaret Thatcher
On its front. On the outside, she says this:
"I know you don't want to have another birthday"
And on the inside she says this:
"But nothing can be done about it."

She was right, of course, but how we respond
Is up to us. We can follow Mrs. Thatcher
And accept Old Age with Stoic resignation.
We can rebel and rage heroically against it.
Or we can follow my Aunt Helen, a humorist
Right to the end. "The highlight of my day,"
She used to say, "is when the metamucil kicks in."

Aunt Helen was right, too.

THE VOICE

The older you get, the stronger the urge
To stay home and do nothing.
"Let's not go," the voice whispers
As you pack for the long-planned trip.
"It's too complicated, too uncertain."

You go anyway, and you're proud of yourself
When you return. "I did it," you think.
Yet the voice persists. When you're planning
A day trip to the city, an hour away,
It still whispers "It's too much trouble."

And even when you decide to go out
For coffee, a fifteen minute drive, the voice
Reminds you that parking may be difficult.

Perhaps old age is simply following the voice,
But I know people much older than me
Who still go out for coffee, and a sweet.

BEING RETIRED

JOB DONE

I turned in my office key today.
There was no more work to do.
I felt nothing more than done.

It was a moment I'd imagined,
Thought about, for years:
How would I feel when I gave up
My one small private niche,
Where my books and pictures,
Even my battered coffee maker,
Were proof it was I
Who lived and worked in that space
And had good reason to be there?

I enjoyed this job for half a century.
How can I walk away from it with no sadness,
No wistful looking back?
When the job is finished, you move on -
That's what the old guys say,
And that, I guess, is what I've done.

THE CONTRACT

I didn't want to retire.
I worked ten years longer than I had to.
To me, retirement was old guys
In baseball caps, with bellies
Like beachballs, or a foursome
Of fat, slow-moving guys
Puttering around in golfcarts.
To me, retirement looked like a deal
Too good to be true, a contract
You signed and then couldn't escape:
You got a life with nothing
You had to do but eat and sleep;
You gave up a life of challenge
And meaning and purpose.

And then my employer
Made me an offer I just couldn't refuse,
And there I was, retired, living
The life without challenge and meaning
And purpose I had long despised.

And, you know, it's kind of fun.

SEPTEMBER SONG

This September feels a little strange
There's no work to return to.
It hasn't been summer vacation;
It's just been summer.

But summer is different now.
It no longer ends on September first.
The glorious weather is still here,
And we can live in it daily,
Not just on weekends.

The weekdays belong to us.
Things are still open, but the people
Are gone. Except for us, the shops are empty.
We can walk into any restaurant
And get a good table.

But what we like most
Is just being outside in September,
Wandering around with no real purpose,
Admiring the gardens and old houses,
Enjoying the perfect weather.

And, when we want
A little more excitement, it's easy
Enough to find it. Tuesday is half-price day
For seniors at the Cumberland Fair.
We plan to be there.

THE QUESTION

Everybody asks me.
It's what you ask a retired person.
They don't mean any harm by it,
And I never take offense,

But do you remember how you felt
When you'd been married just a year
Or so and people started asking,
"When are you going to start a family?"
Or when you were trying to finish
A project which was already late,
A project that nagged you
Night and day, and somebody
Would ask you, "When are you ever
Going to finish that thing?"?

That's how I feel when people ask me,
"What are you doing with yourself now?"

TO FREEDOM

A friend of mine pounded the table
And said "I'm retiring."
He'd made a good case for it:
His office needed an overhaul;
He didn't want to fire people he liked.
But when he proposed a toast "To Freedom,"
I just couldn't raise my glass.

Few of us are ready to retire.
I certainly wasn't, and my friend wasn't either.
He wanted to write something (Don't we all!).
Beyond that, he really had no plans.
He wanted to be free and, yes,
You are free of your former work.
But you're not carefree, free of all cares.

When you get up in the morning
With nothing on your schedule,
Retirement can feel like freedom.
It can also feel like drifting in the ocean
With no shore in sight.

MONDAY MORNING

On Monday morning, you have to feel good
About being retired.

No matter how much you liked your work
(And I liked mine a lot),
You walked to the office on Monday morning
With a heavy heart.

But, when you're retired, Monday morning
Gives you a boost.
You get a whole wide-open stretch of time,
A world of choices.

Even if you squandered the previous week,
And the one before that,
And the one before that, you always get
A whole new start.

SEASONS

There are times in New England
When it's hard to tell the season.
The sun is bright but not warm.
The grass is green but not growing.
There are no leaves on the trees.
Is it April or November?

For an old guy,
Retiring feels the same way.
He knows it's really November,
But sometimes it feels like Spring,
And sometimes it feels like both seasons
At the same time.

ROUTINES

BALANCING ACT

There's always some old guy
Older than you, some old guy
You can pretend to feel sorry for.
"Look at that old codger –
He can barely move," while you,
Of course, are Jack B. Nimble himself.

Except in the morning. Where's Jack then,
When, with one sock on,
You contemplate how far away
An old guy's foot can grow;
Or when you're standing there, balancing,
One foot already in its place,
And contemplating the final task –
The quick lift, the hopeful downward thrust?

EVERY MORNING

Every morning, for an hour or two,
The old guy works through the morning paper,
Solving the world's problems.

Why does he bother?
He's an old guy sitting in a small-town restaurant.
Nobody cares what he thinks.

Only he cares, the guy himself.
He sits there alone, working with his mind,
Making the world make sense.

BREAKFAST

For breakfast, I have two choices.

I can stay home and my wife
Will prepare it. She'll boil an egg
Just long enough. She'll bring me
Juice, toast, coffee, my pills.
Then we'll sit together at the counter,
Sharing plans for the day.
After years of rushing out the door,
It's good to have the time.
(Later, I'll do the dishes, just so you know.)

And then, some mornings, I'll throw on
Old clothes, drive down to Rick's,
Sit down with the other old guys
And shoot the shit. That's good, too.

COAT AND TIE

What am I going to do with all these clothes –
These sport jackets, dress pants, white shirts, ties?
These were my uniform, the things I wore every day.
Now, I have to hunt for places to wear them.
I could get by with just my dark suit.

I know I could give these things away,
But I can't do that just yet. They help me
Remember occasions that mattered, good times
And bad. And when something new comes up,
They give me plenty of options.

Nobody wears a coat and tie
Any more. In situations where every man
Used to wear them, I'm often the only one left.
But I don't mind being a relic from days
Gone by. In fact, I rather enjoy it.

I can wear a coat and tie
Into any nice restaurant or theater
And be perfectly at ease. Nobody will point or stare.
And, for special occasions, when casual attire
Won't suffice, I'm back in my element.

SKUNKS

We have a skunk problem.
A skunk has taken residence
Somewhere beneath our house.
Not every night, but most nights,
The skunk makes his presence known.
When we open the bedroom door,
The smell assaults us in the hall.
It can be strong (though almost always
Gone by noon) and it bothers us a lot,
Especially my wife. When I spray
The anti-varmint potion we bought
At the hardware store, the varmint
Just moves to another spot
In our large, cluttered cellar.

I'm less bothered than my wife is.
I wish the skunk were gone,
But I think I know where he's coming from.
He's acting like an old guy does:
He gets up, passes some gas, and goes about
His business. It's not that big a deal.

PLACES

HOME TOWN

When you're working, the world outside
Your work, outside your head,
Is like a quaint little town you drive through
On the way to the office.

When you're retired, you can visit the place,
Walk through the streets,
Take a long, unhurried look at the houses
You just glanced at.

You can sit down at the local restaurant
And talk with the people
You used to notice as you drove by,
Get to know them a little.

You feel like you're visiting for the first time,
But it's the town where your house is.
You weren't really living here; you were just passing
Through. Now, you can stay.

THE LOCALS

I left the house at 7 and got back at 9.
I was having breakfast at Rick's.
I sat at a table with three old guys, three locals,
And they talked about how this town
Used to be, and what it was like to grow up here.
Right after they left, two more old guys,
Also locals, sat down at the same table
And we all talked for another hour.

They were angry and blasted the voters
For being uninformed. I agreed, but,
Since my side won this time, I wasn't that upset.
Still, I don't like to win when the locals lose.
I know my rights are equal to theirs,
But it doesn't seem quite fair.

BUCKET LIST

I don't have a bucket list.
I've seen some famous places and hope
To see more, but I also want plenty of time
To visit little unknown places
Where not much happens.

In a Scottish town by the sea,
I watched two young mothers pushing
Their prams over an ancient stone road.
It was a sunny morning and
Not a car went by.

I watched for a good while,
Then walked down to the harbor.
The sea was calm and even the seabirds were quiet.
The only sound was a carpenter's hammer
Off in the distance.

That was forty years ago,
And I still remember how young
And comfortable those two mothers seemed,
How deep that silence was, how the sound
Of that hammer echoed.

SEATS

As our motorcoach passes
Through the ancient town square,
I see an old man sitting
On a bench beneath the trees.
There are autumn leaves
In the grass around him and
On the cobblestone road.
With his woolen jacket and cap,
He could have been sitting there
Two centuries ago.

No open shops, no other people.
The old man sits there by himself,
Motionless, looking straight ahead
At nothing in particular.
"Boy, I wouldn't want to be him,"
Says the guy across the aisle.
For me, I'm not so sure.
He's sitting in his ancestors' home.
We're sitting in a tour bus.

At the Resort

This resort was built for the people
With Old Money, the ones who stayed
For the whole season and brought
Their servants with them.

Not many of that type around here now -
Maybe a tweedy old guy or two. Most of the guests
Look like they made their own money
And intend to get their money's worth.

We're using our own money, too,
But all these things feel like treats to us:
Hot breakfast served in the room,
Fresh white robes for the pool,
Afternoon high tea.

Nobody can take such things
For granted. Nobody can earn them.
Having the money to buy such things
Is itself a gift. The only proper
Sentiment is gratitude.

CHILDREN

FAMILY RESTAURANT

We're in a family pizza restaurant –
Lots and lots of children. Every table
Has a kid or two, a young mother
And, usually, a young father, too.
It's a charming scene. The kids don't fight
With each other; they jabber away
At their parents, or draw with crayons
On the paper tablecloths. The parents
Appear to be interested. They sit and smile.

The whole scene makes me wonder.
Did our little family ever look like this?
All I remember is how tedious it was,
How bad I was at playing the young father,
How I hated the whining and fussing,
How I tried and failed to control it,
How I'd suggest that we lock the kids
Outside in the car and eat in peace,
How my wife would never agree.

Still, I've become a lot more patient.
I find young children quite interesting now.
Perhaps, if I had a second chance, I could be
Like one of these smiling young fathers.

Too old for it, though.   Thank God.

OLD GROUCH

Children appear in summer,
Like mosquitoes and black flies.
They overrun our parks,
Our beaches, our city squares.
They scream for the sport of it.
Their high, sharp voices
Could slice through steel.
And they run, always run,
Spreading the screaming around,
Filling our quiet adult spaces
With raucous noise.

Their parents are worthless,
Sitting there chatting and drinking,
Ignoring the chaos around them.
All we can do is wait for fall,
When children are locked in
Their schools, controlled
Once more by professionals,
And we will filter back
Into our spaces, reclaim our benches,
And feed the docile pigeons,
Who are slow and quiet, making
Only an occasional coo.

BABIES

To be perfectly honest, I'm not that fond
Of babies. I hate it when they cry. I'd rather
Listen to a chain saw than to a crying baby.
When I watch otherwise sane women
Fussing and squealing over a fuzzy-haired
Human in a carriage or crib, I'm mystified:
What makes them do it, and why
Do almost all of them do it?

But, lo and behold, I've found a baby
I actually like, my chiropractor's son.
This little fellow never stops smiling.
He's so cheerful, so delightful to watch
And listen to, that I find myself coming
To the office early to see if he's awake.
And I even find myself waving to him
And talking in nonsensical ways.

I must be getting senile.

KIDS

My grandson, ten years old,
Was walking home, and we watched him
From the front window. He was in no hurry
To see us. He was wielding a big stick,
Speaking aloud to each pole or tree,
Then whacking it with sword strokes.
He worked his way slowly up the street,
Unaware of us adults in the window,
A kid in a kid's world, and we could only
Watch him and smile.

I thought of my grandson yesterday.
I was riding my bicycle and there was nowhere
I really had to be. Everything felt good:
The warm sun, the smooth asphalt,
The effortless glide of the tires.
I couldn't help swerving my front wheel
Back and forth, just for the fun of it,
And I found I was singing away, quite loudly,
Unaware that I'd been singing at all.

I wasn't winning the Tour de France –
Only a real kid could imagine that.
But I did get a little closer to my grandson,
At least for a while.

Sixth Grade

These girls have had a great weekend.
They arrived, jumped into the ocean,
And spent most of their days there,
Coming out in the evenings for barbecues,
Badminton, and long, deep sleep.

On Sunday afternoon, it's time for them
To pile into the car and go home,
Back to the sixth grade, to homework
Not yet done, to a normal bedtime,
A normal sleep, and an early rising.

I picture them on Monday morning
Trudging to the bus stop in the near-dark,
Dreading the day's required tasks.
I can still remember that same trudge,
That same child's impulse to resist.

I felt that impulse for seventy years,
Every morning of my school and working life.
It disappeared the day I retired.

What a long, long journey I've taken.
What a long road these girls have before them.
I hope the world will be kind.

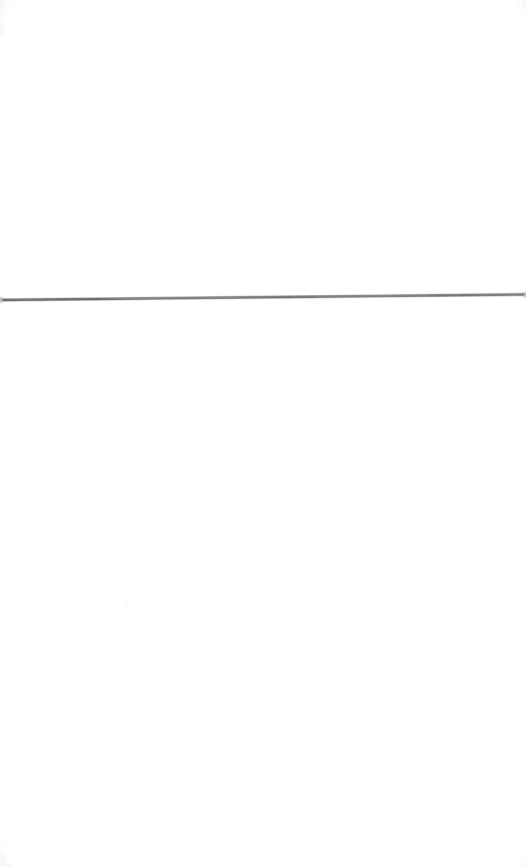

FAMILY

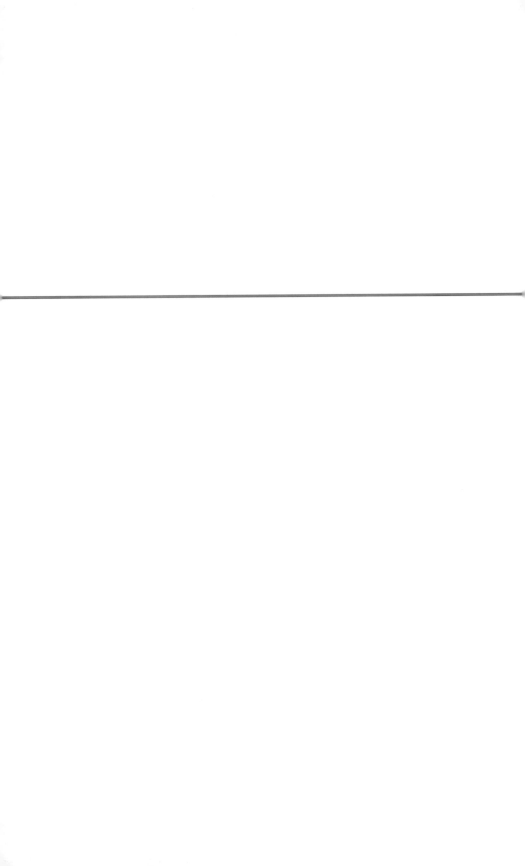

GROWN-UPS

My children are in their fifties now.
I don't see them all that often, and don't hear
From them for weeks on end. After a while,
One of us will break down and we'll talk
On the phone. I'm comfortable enough
With the way things are between me and them.
They have busy lives and I know, more or less,
What they're up to. They don't worry about me,
And they don't have to: at this point,
There's nothing to worry about.

We try to get together for major holidays.
My wife and I get down to visit each of them
Once or twice a year. When we get together,
It's lively and pleasant. We argue sometimes,
But never fight seriously (although Bush/Gore
Over Thanksgiving was a little tense).
On Father's Day, they usually call, but not
Always. I'm pleased when they do, not upset
When they don't. Likewise with my birthday.
I don't care about the small stuff.

I don't want command performances.
I don't want to be called out of duty, or guilt.
My children and I get along fine.
When we're together, we enjoy each other's
Company. When they need help, I try
To give it, and, when I really need them,
They're always right here.

HALF THE BAY

My grandfather liked to tell the story.
His father, eighty-five years old,
Looked out at the bay behind the house
And said: "You know, Tony,
I bet I drank this much wine in my life."
It was something to consider.

The old man had grown up in the old country,
Where they start their wine-drinking young,
And kept at it when he got to the States.
He'd centered much of his life on wine,
Drinking it, and also making it himself.
He'd be down in my grandfather's cellar,
Mashing and heating and bottling.
Word got around, and other old men
Would join him, including the police chief,
My grandfather said.

His mistakes were family legend.
The cellar ceiling was stained red
From the bottles, capped too soon,
Which popped their corks and exploded.
Hundreds of bottles had left their marks,
Those, of course, were the exceptions.
Most of the bottles had settled down
And ended up inside the winemaker.

So, he'd drunk a lot of wine.
Not enough to fill the whole bay, I suppose,
But maybe half the bay.

THE WAVE

I'm wearing my hair longer now.
Long white hair on an old guy can look good.
It can also hide your bald spot.
When my hair gets long enough,
I can comb it from the front
And a wave will magically appear.
It makes me look like a guy from the thirties,
Someone like my father,
Who was, in fact, a guy from the thirties
And who had, in the old college photos,
A head of long and wavy hair.

He wore it short during his working years.
When he was older and retired,
He let it grow and the magic wave returned.
His long hair stayed with him to the end –
No bald spots for my old man -
And the last picture I have of him
Is of a dapper old man lying in state,
His eyes closed, his hair long and silver,
And, in the front of it, a wave.

MY MOTHER

My mother has always been
Twenty-five years older than me.
She keeps ahead of me, consistently.
No matter how hard I live,
I never close the gap.

Not that I want to.
I like to see her out there in front.
She's over a hundred now, still on her own,
Still showing me, and all of us,
How it can be done.

What's in a Name?

My mother doesn't write out her checks
Anymore, but she still wants to sign them.
I point out the line for her, and she slowly
    Writes her name somewhere near it.
        My mother is a very old woman
            (She's an old guy's mother!),
        And she can't really see the line.
            She just tries to go straight.
    Sometimes the signature slants up;
Sometimes it slants down. More often
        Than not, it's right on the line.

        My mother writes slowly, as if
        Inscribing each letter in stone,
    Yet her signature is always clear.
        It always tells us who she is.

HUSBAND AND WIFE

SURPRISE

It's always a shock
When you look across the room
And notice a pretty woman,
A stylish, middle-aged woman
Talking with her friends,
A lively, charming woman
You'd enjoy talking with, too,
And maybe even connecting with,
If she and you were free;
And then you watch her
Walk over and take the hand
Of an old guy with white hair,
Her husband apparently, but
Old enough to be her father.

If you happen to notice my wife,
The old guy will be me.

DRIVING MRS. C.

I can sense,
From your stifled cries,
And from your white knuckles
Clutching the door handle,
That my driving makes you uneasy.

Slow drivers do irk me,
And, yes, I tend to shout obscenities
While driving a foot behind them.
But they never hear the stuff I shout,
And I haven't hit one yet.

At least I don't drive
Like my father did. When turning left
He'd cut several car-lengths off the corner.
My mother's white knuckles would
Make yours look pink.

I will admit to one fault:
I tend to fall asleep at the wheel.
And sometimes I'll start a little argument
With my sweet wife just to stay awake.
Sorry about that, Dear.

HER OLD MAN

Poor woman. How does she stand it?
How does she stand this bumbling, undependable,
Utterly predictable old man?

He is never on time.
He forgets what she says, refuses
His seat belt, snaps at her for nothing -
What a trial to live with!

He's bored with his own self.
How can she not be bored with him, too?
How can she smile at him in a genuine way,
Even enjoy his company?

Because he's her old man,
Because she sees in him something
Of value, something he, too, once saw clearly,
And wants him to realize it's still there.

ANOTHER PERSON

Way up ahead of me, my wife
Is riding her bike, really moving.

It's strange to see her from a distance.
We're almost always together. Her smile
Is the first thing I see in the morning,
The last thing I see at night.
I know this woman better than any person
I've ever known, and she knows me as well.
Yet, even at those times when we seem
To be speaking each other's thoughts,
There is still a space between us.
She's another person, a mystery
I can never solve, and so am I to her.

She rides ahead of me, really moving.
I have to work hard to keep her in view.

CONVERSATIONS

At the next table,
Two young businessmen
Are having a working lunch, making
A "risk assessment inventory"
(So they called it) for a new project.
Listening to their earnest talk
Reminds me of my own working days.

At another table, a little girl
Has been peaking at us from behind
Her napkin. When we peak back,
She hides her face. With her black hair,
She reminds me of how my own daughter
(Now at the height of her career)
Used to look. "Three?" I ask my wife.
"Closer to two. She's still in diapers,"
My wife replies. "Yeah," I say,
"But maybe just when they go out."
"That could be," she says.

WIDOWS

There's no good word for a male widow,
But I was one once, and I still remember
How painful it was. Weekends were the worst.
With no one and nothing to come home to.
I remember sitting in a silent house,
Then lying awake in a double bed,
Imagining intruders at the door.
Most of all, I remember being cut off
From my own past, carrying in my mind
Years and years of memories
That could never be shared.

That was my taste of widowhood,
And I still recall it when I visit my new wife
(New as of 30 years) at her place of work.
She works among widows, the only woman
With a living husband, and visiting her there
Makes me uneasy, as if my presence
Might cause the others pain.

I'm sure the others wish us well,
And no doubt women deal with widowhood
Better than hapless males like me.
Still, the sight of an older couple
Still together could make any widow sigh,
Any widow -- female, or male.

PORTRAITS

STRANGERS

Maybe I'm lucky, or maybe
I'm old enough to draw their pity,
But people are nice to me.
When I'm schlepping my suitcase
Up the subway stairs, a young woman
(A young woman!) grabs it out
Of my hand and brings it to the top.
When I'm standing on the sidewalk,
Looking lost, some stranger comes up
To show me the way.
And the people who work in stores
Are courteous and helpful.
"Do you have any spoons?" I ask
The barista. "Certainly, sir,
I'll go get one for you."
And the clerk at the supermarket
Takes the stupid reusable bag my wife
Makes me carry, fills it neatly
With all my groceries, and hands
It to me with a smile.

Has it always been like this, or
Was I just too busy to notice?

No Hurry

Driving around town this morning,
I was cut off by two cars.

The first was a white Volvo.
It came out of the library parking lot
And cut right in front of me.
The driver was a very old man,
Clutching the wheel with both hands
And staring straight ahead.
He never saw me.

The second was an old Chevy
Coming out of the convenience store.
The driver was a middle-aged woman
In a gray sweatshirt. She saw me
At the last minute and pumped her brakes,
But she was already past.
I waved her on.

For years, I've blown my horn
At any driver that crossed me. This time,
I wasn't even annoyed. I figured those two
Had better reasons to use that road
Than I did. I'm not in a big hurry
Any more. I can wait
A minute.

IN THE AUDIENCE

The world is full of talented young people-
Singers and actors, painters and writers.
They're talented, but they'll never be known,
Never make a living. They'll wait on tables
A few years, then drift away to find
A real job. Their bleak future is certain.

That's the official view, but the old guy
Who sits in the audience applauding can see
Beyond it. He can understand these kids,
Who don't give a damn about the future,
Who choose to do what they want to do
For as long as they can.

DAN

We were having a pleasant breakfast,
Two old buddies, Dan and I,
Sitting by the window in the sun.
Dan was weaker now and speaking softly,
And the fussing baby near-by made him
Hard to hear. I was getting annoyed.

In the corner of that restaurant
There were five people, four of them
Unhappy, all of us but Dan,
Who smiled and waved at the baby,
Spoke kind words to the anxious parents,
And made us all feel better.

Dan always made people feel better.
That was how he was.

WHAT WE GET TO KEEP

When Bob showed up for tennis
Wearing a faded yellow sweater
With moth-holes as big as quarters in it,
We knew right away that something
Must be wrong.

And when we found out
His wife had died over the winter,
We weren't surprised. She would never
Have let him out of the house
Looking like that.

But there he was,
Playing tennis well into his eighties.
He couldn't move quickly, but he could still
Hit the ball hard, with a firm wrist
And a short, crisp swing.

He'd been club champion
Once, and beneath that ragged sweater
Was a technique most of us will never master.
We pitied the man for his heavy loss,
And wondered at his skill.

Given a choice, of course,
He would rather have kept his wife.
But we don't have much choice as to what we lose
And what we get to keep.

PARTNERS

An old guy and his dog:
The guy shuffling along, barely moving,
His eyes fixed on the ground in front;
The dog frisky, ready to run,
Prancing, pulling at the leash.

Different, yet connected:
Like a teacher and his disciple,
Like a father and an eager child,
Like the aging body and the ageless soul.

OLD MAN ABOUT TOWN

Had I been born in Italy
And stayed in Agropoli, the little town
Where my family owned a house, I would be
An old man shuffling around the town square.

I would be wearing a suit coat, always,
A good shirt with a collar, sometimes a tie,
Dress pants with cuffs, and leather shoes.
On cold days, a wool cap; on Sundays, a fedora.

I would be walking slowly, inspecting the shops,
Or sitting at a table with the other old men,
Talking and sipping coffee. And, every day,
I would sit by myself on my favorite bench.

I would sit there for a while every single day.
I wonder what I would be thinking.

EPILOGUE

APOLOGY

Many topics related to old age
Have been omitted from this volume.
Pain, for instance, and illness.
Death and dying. Hospitals.
Nursing homes. Loss of loved ones,
Loss of memory, loss of hope.
These and other topics have been
Deferred until <u>Old Guy, Part Two</u>,
Which I don't intend to write.

CPSIA information can be obtained at www.ICGtesting.com
Printed in the USA
BVOW02s2028140116

432930BV00003B/112/P